Yes Lif

Photo by Scott Dawson

Dominic Berry is a Manchester-based performance poet whose work has taken him across the continents of Europe, North and South America, Asia and Australasia. He has won Manchester Literature Festival's Superheroes of Slam and New York's Nuyorican Poets' Café Slam, and been Glastonbury Festival's Poet in Residence. He has also twice been publicly voted Saboteur Awards' Best Spoken Word Performer.

"From hilarious, heart-warming poems dedicated to He-Man's bum to the wonders of friendship and community, the poems come alive off the page and aim directly for the feels."
Desree, Glastonbury Festival poet-in-residence 2022

"Dominic's sharp wit, keen observation and wonderful energy make his poetry equally joyful and moving."
Joe Sellman-Leava, writer & performer

"Dominic sets out a welcome mat with the simplest of words before drenching you with complicated humanity. Experience the wildest, most brutal honesty in the safest, gentlest of hands."
Scott Tyrrell, stand-up poet

"Humble, heartfelt and triumphant. He writes with contagious enthusiasm and zest for life. The themes in Dominic's writing are so universal and accessible, it feels like he's sharing your story too."
Victoria Shineman, poet

"He sees the world differently, and through his words, maybe we can see it that way too, if only for a little while."
Culain Wood, poet

"Beautiful writing. A sharp, unflinching eye."
John McGrath, Manchester International Festival Artistic Director

"Robust, intelligent and uncompromising ... deeply poetic. The searing honesty which is the mark of every true poet shines out of every line."
Write Out Loud

"Hilarious and moving ... crackles with energy and humanity."
Tim Clare, poet

"Whether he is fiercely flying the flag for vegans or proudly probing into the politics of sexuality, he does so with a smile on his face and a fire in his gut."
Sara Hirsch, UK Poetry Slam Champion

DOMINIC BERRY
YES LIFE

Flapjack Press

flapjackpress.co.uk
Exploring the synergy between performance and the page

Published in 2022 by Flapjack Press
Salford, Gtr Manchester
⊕ flapjackpress.co.uk f Flapjack Press
🐦 flapjackpress ▶ Flapjack Press

ISBN 978-1-8384703-5-7

Cover photo by Scott Dawson

Printed by Imprint Digital
Exeter, Devon
⊕ digital.imprint.co.uk

MANCHESTER
A UNESCO City
of Literature

Dedicated to my amazing Aunt Julie.

Your passion, political activism, poetic talent and powerful presence inspire me. I love you and thank you for bringing brilliant light to my life.

Contents

Fantasy   **12**
Haiku for Dreams   13
Festival Fever   14
The Crying Café   16
Fantastic Fright   18
Acceptable Anger   20
Ode to Blanka from Street Fighter 2   22
He-Man, The Most Powerful Bottom in the Universe   24
Playground Fantasy   25

Reality   **26**
Haiku for Love   27
Choose-Your-Own-Adventure   28
Romance for a He-Man   30
The Business Behind He-Man   32
Did Boris Johnson Become the Modern He-Man?   34
Why These Songs Matter   36
Ali and Zain   38
And James Lived Happily Ever After   40

Isolation   **42**
Haiku for Loss   43
8-Bit Buddy   44
Video Games Don't Hurt Me   46
Pantoum for Possibilities   48
People Like Shit   50
Five Days Dreaming of Sleep   52
Goodbye, Anxiety   56
Love in the Sea   58

Companionship   **60**
Haiku for Friends   61
Sestina for Friends   62
My Friend, Online   64
Warmth: A Poem About a Pandemic   66
My Northern Soul   67
From a Glastonbury Mosh Pit   68
Glastonbury Mud   70
Ghazal for Possibilities   72
High-fiving Tree Branches   73
Rondeau for When I'm Low   74
Sonnet for Shell   75
A Frisbee   76
Like Puppies   78
I Am   80
My Friend, Sleep   82
Haiku for a New Season   85

Acknowledgements

This collection has been written with the experience gained from being a student of tae kwon-do. I would like to acknowledge and thank Master Iqbal, all the senior instructors and everyone I've met through the United Tae kwon-do Organisation. An oath we take is to 'build a more peaceful world'. Being a student of tae kwon-do gives my life great purpose and joy.

In 2021, I met Luiz. I feel grateful for the wonderful time we spent discussing poems. He says no one owns an idea, but I know many of these poems would not be here without the exciting suggestions he made during our delightful days together.

I acknowledge and deeply thank the people who join Luiz in having poems dedicated to them in the latter half of *Yes Life*. Graeme, Scott, Josh, Michelle, Nick and Ian, you are wonderful and I love you.

Finally, thank you mum. You made the foundations of where I am and who I am today. I owe you so much, and I love you more than words can say.

Dominic Berry
June 2022

Yes Life

Fantasy

Haiku for Dreams

Is love possible?
Let imagined magic spark
and dreams spring to life.

Festival Fever

My fantasy of joy. A rewrite of a poem called 'Sizzling', which I originally wrote as Glastonbury Festival Poet in Residence.

Didn't need sleep.
Embracing flaming fantasies,
we were loved-up lunatics.
Bare skin invited fire.
Our delighted dancing
woke stars.

For days,
the sun kept flirting with us
'cos the sun thought we were fit.
The sun wanted us to strip,
so we did!
Naked.
Amazingly mud-kissed.

Some stomachs are washboards.
Some bellies beachball.
All are beautifully dirty-clean.

Smooth.
Hairy.
Fat.
Skinny.
Scarred.
Sexy.

We held this bliss on open lips
until sunlight was dwindling ...

and then
we kept on glistening,
even after dark!

We eventually slept
with a mindful of molten miracles
and a glorious grin.
Dionysian dreams
rekindling.
For even in the softest shadows of sleep,
we were still
sizzling.

The Crying Café
My fantasy of sadness.

Maybe I'm strange, but I want to ask whether
I'm the only one who wishes more people cried together?

I see such sadness in the world
and I often want to weep.
Don't only mean lonely, subtle sniffles.
I mean loud howls in a crowd.
Sometimes my tears won't wait.
Don't drop privately.
They burst out publicly
embarrassing me,
but I know I need to let this upset out.
No doubt,
and there should be no shame
if we don't aim
to keep these feelings locked away.

So,
this is my pitch for a Crying Café.

Imagine somewhere
we could all be audibly bawling,
sharing our troubles,
sharing a table,
sat at a Crying Café.

If you'd rather be smiling, OK,
there are already plenty of other places for that,
but if weeping is where you are currently at,
let's make a date at a Crying Café!

A Crying Café. A Crying Café.
We could open one up today.
Take me away to a Crying Café;
a welcoming space
for the wettest face
where we could embrace
grief with grace.
Oh! Let's go
for some bleary-eyed, snotty-nosed
tissue soaking.
I am not joking.
I would sincerely love a place
where we could all sob safely.
Fairly trade sorrows
over the flattest flat white.
No sweetener needed.
A cathartic cuppa
with caring comrades.

No one trying to correct us.
It's not bad to be sad.
Everyone accepts us.
No one saying *"You're over-reacting"*.
Just kind and mindful interacting.

We wouldn't need loyalty cards, because here
we could gain the greatest rewards:
being
together. Feeling.
Together. Healing.
Together. Weeping
where no one would ever have to hide

and we could leave with loving connections,
feeling closer having cried.

Fantastic Fright
My fantasy of fear.

There is fantastic fright in Hollywood horror,
roller-coaster rides, sky-diving, rock-climbing,
ghost trains,
and gory video games.
I find them phenomenally fun,
focused fully on the thrilling present time.
I cry sublime screams
between
delighted
smiles.

The same is not true
when I meet someone new.
I try to smile, but inside
I am screaming,
and these screams don't feel sublime.
Here
is phantasmic fear.

With new people, I am not even real.
My body may seem to be there,
but my mind is rewinding,
playing proper horror
of every person who ever gave me grief.
When I meet a potential new friend or lover,
I measure them against every other
earlier hurt, vicious and vast,
given by people from my past.

Then,
I fast-forward to a future
where prophecies of pain
claim all my worst moments will happen again.

But I don't want to be mangled
by these movies in my brain.
Not frozen in future fear,
I want to be here.
Tell me how
can I be now?

I can do it with a scary sport or game.
With you, I only have one aim.

I want this current moment to be yours and mine,
so how can I focus fully on this present time?

Acceptable Anger
My fantasy of the fourth of what some folks call 'The Four Core Emotions'.

You throw the controller away from you
when I beat you at Street Fighter 2.
You have rage which cannot be tamed
when we play a video game.
Countless times, I've seen
you hurl swearwords at the screen,
screaming merry hell.

You don't take defeat very well!

But I am glad your anger isn't repressed.
Emotions are healthier when expressed.

We agree it is OK to be
venting ire through fantasy.
I know you often do this.
You are very clear on that.
You say it's OK
because this is your flat;
but anger in public ...?
You say that's wrong.
That's *inappropriate*.
That is *not on*.

Protesters are marching,
raising painted banners.
You quickly dismiss them
as just having bad manners.
Label a public maddened mood
as *inconsiderate, disruptive* and *rude*.

Why is it acceptable to get angry at fantasy,
but such a taboo to be riled by reality?

Is it *inconsiderate* for some people to be
visibly angry by the world they see?

The government is lying,
trying to cut services to the most needy
whilst giving cash handouts to the most greedy.
The poor stay poor.
The rich, oh so rich.
Billionaires turn on charm like a Nintendo switch.

If life is like a game
can we correct this unfair glitch?

What can we do
to help our heavy world get lighter?

How can we face injustice
with the passion of a Street Fighter?

Ode to Blanka from Street Fighter 2

The first of two consecutive 'rude' poems. In the 1990s video game, Street Fighter 2, Blanka is a character in a tournament, fighting to beat all the other challengers (many of whom are named in this poem) and eventually face The Mighty Bison, the game's fearsome final opponent.

Whilst Guile's smile's not my style,
Zangief's beef is best left sheathed,
and whilst Ken's bottom might seem tighter,
you're the sexiest street fighter.

You're the sexiest street fighter.
Pale males fail. Green's brighter.
Grab my joystick, pull it all night,
exciting, biting, lightning enticer.

Nicer than a slicing from Vega's claws.
Far nicer than the "Tiger" that Sagat roars.
Splatter me with flattery. No cause to pause.
The sexiest street fight, with your

big howls and growls. Such feral calls.
Such special moves. Those rolling balls
just can't improve. You've got it all.
Oh, Blanka! How your drool enthrals.

Oh, Blanka! How you strike me dumb.
I love to watch you scratch your bum.
Please, let me kiss your bulging tum.
Oh, Blanka! Blanka! Let me come

into your arms, into your game.
Don't be alarmed when I proclaim
I love your snarls, your teeth, your name,
your orange chest hairs' raging flame.

Conduct your volts. Bolt through me, Blanka.
In this thunder, be my anchor.
You'll feel richer than a banker.
Drop your shorts and let me spank ya!

You're the boss. Your beast technique's
enormous power is unique.
With animal skills you can't put a price on,
you're so much bigger than any Bison.

He-Man, The Most Powerful Bottom in the Universe

The second of two consecutive 'rude' poems, and the first of many featuring He-Man. He-Man was a once-popular superhero in cartoons and toy lines in the early 1980s. His evil rival was Skeletor, and the TV show they were in was called *Masters of the Universe*. This poem is a true story.

When I was young, my mum knew I was gay
from one specific thing I drew one day.
I proudly showed my mum what I had done.
A crayon drawing showing He-Man's bum.

A gift for which I craved my mother's thanks
where Skeletor was giving He-Man spanks,
for not a single thing could make me cheerier
than drawing villains whacking that posterior.

My mum said … … "Oooh, that's nice," and I confess
her praise made me feel such a great success,
and when the neighbours came, she would not flinch
with He-Man's bare bum stuck upon our fridge.

Playground Fantasy

If I could make only one of my many fantasies come true, this would
be the one.

I wish I could go back in time to tell ten-year-old me
it is OK to be a big, girly boy.

I want to tell him, "You will find joy
in effeminacy *and* masculinity.
Reject the fragility of male identity.
You will find as much affinity
in the daring drag of David Bowie
and the silver lipstick of Tricky
as you currently do in admiring
the macho muscle of He-Man
and all the other boys' toys
which are great to enjoy
but you have so much more about you
than a plastic action figure or cartoon.
One day, you will find room to grow
and know the fecundity of gender fluidity."

And I know,
ten-year-old me would say,
"What do all those long words mean?"

And I would reply,
"They mean, I've seen those playground lads
leave you lonely, feeling strange,
but I have also seen your future.
It gets better.
The world will change."

Reality

Haiku for Love

Tell me love will come.
Please, light my dark mind. Don't say,
like summer, love fades.

Choose-Your-Own-Adventure

As a child, these books were a joyful way to spend time.

Life is not a linear novel.
No fixed middle or end.
Our lives are full of choices.
I have chosen to say poems I've penned.
More than once or twice,
I have written poems which give advice:
    "Don't blame others for mistakes,
    take responsibility,
    choose positivity."

You see, I have believed
in the power of our own choices
ever since I was a kid,
ever since I hid my head in
choose-your-own-adventure books.

In choose-your-own-adventure books,
you, the reader, choose what to do
and the end of the story is determined by you.
Act without wisdom, go to page 92:
        You lose!
Act honourably, go to page 63:
        You succeed!
I felt powerful devouring these stories,
so mum bought them all for me ...

but I know I never chose to be born
healthy, able-bodied, white, British male,
in a home full of books
and with a mother's love that never failed.

I grew up with someone who cared,
someone who was always there.

When others have tried to tell me
that their lives are more challenged than mine,
I have often interrupted to tell them
good choices can make it all fine ...

but if my life was a choose-your-own-adventure,
my first pages were written by my mother.

If all of our lives are choose-your-own-adventures,
some books have more choices within them than others.

Romance for a He-Man

First poem in my 'He-Man Reality Trilogy'. Teela, Evil Lyn and Stratos are three characters in He-Man's cartoon, *Masters of the Universe*.

When I was ten, alone in my room,
I loved my Saturday morning cartoons.

I saw He-Man with Teela.
They were in a romance.
Like Teela, I admired
He-Man's tiny, furry pants.

Was Teela the warrior woman of He-Man's dreams?
A couple of confident heroes. Super-strong, it seemed.

Woman and man.
Spick and span.
Wholesome and clean.
Never obscene.

When I was ten,
no cartoons showed men
with other men.

Would seeing gays in cartoons have been right?
I've heard some say seeing such a sight
might turn kids queer,
but listen here,
seeing He-Man and Teela together
never made me straight.

It was not great, not seeing anyone like me
reflected on my screen.

I don't mean I should have seen sex.

I mean affection.

So, when I played games,
I chose to make a little plot correction.
I made my beloved He-Man toy
and my feather-chested Stratos figure
cuddle.

Two men in tiny, furry pants.
Imaginary romance.
Two loved-up fellas ...
and Teela was not jealous.
Don't worry about Teela.
She could cuddle Evil Lyn.

However, these secret scenarios I savoured
always felt a bit wrong.
Men liking men felt *wrong*.
Me being me felt *wrong*.
If I could see no one else like me,
I must be *wrong*.

Didn't feel mighty.
Didn't feel pride.
Didn't feel like I could share
this longing hidden inside.

Felt shy and insecure.
Believed this was the deal:
The romance of my fantasies
could not be real.

If cartoons had shown
the love for which I longed,
might I have felt like He-Man,
confident and strong?

The Business Behind He-Man

Second poem in my 'He-Man Reality Trilogy'.

Did you know the He-Man cartoon
was the world's first cartoon
made with the main purpose of being an advert
to make even the most adverse
children believe
they needed to retrieve
all seventy-two different He-Man toys?
Retail therapy for little boys.
Hear the television call
"Collect them all!"
Never before was such a vision
carried out with such precision.

My generation
were groomed to be a nation
of failures, to give a big business financial backing.
Kids had to feel like they were lacking
to keep feeding the expanding,
money-making machine.
It was obscene
to let pre-schoolers think they would feel fantastic
if they chose to own every piece of one company's plastic.
Groomed
to consume.
Groomed to be greedy.
Needy.
Feelings of inadequacy
fuelling anxiety.
This became He-Man's curse.

Monetising children's self-worth
because it might stop families striving
to buy so much stuff
if kids thought just being themselves
might be enough.

Did Boris Johnson Become the Modern He-Man?

Third poem in my 'He-Man Reality Trilogy'. I started writing this poem before Boris Johnson was Prime Minister and didn't finish until after he quit.

There are two blond-haired men
who promised to protect their lands.
When Boris was our leader
he had power in his hands.
Did you see Boris break a wall
and call *"Get Brexit done"*?
Like He-Man's fist into our screens;
a comic full of fun.

Now, He-Man used his humour
when he'd laugh with one and all.
Whilst He-Man came from privilege,
he'd stand with tall and small.
The bee people and bird people
he chose to count as friends,
and when there was a conflict
He-Man chose to make amends.

Did Boris break a wall
or did he build more stumbling blocks?
I heard when he compared
a person to a letterbox.
Are piccaninnies and the tank-topped bum-boys
words well used?
When Boris laughed and called this humorous
were we amused?

Some said that Boris did his best,
but He-Man would discuss
should we unite or separate
in groups of *them* and *us*?
I don't think He-Man's just for kids.
Don't cast his ways aside.
As Jo Cox said, "We've more in common
than what could divide."

Why These Songs Matter

A return from my early fantasies with He-Man to what has often been the reality of my romantic life.

First heard in a sweat-wet mirrorballed room,
you are the perfect, euphoric disco tune.
   'I Feel Love'.
I remember the man I kissed that night.
I'd assumed we'd stay together
for more than Summer's reign.
That man is long gone,
but you, the song, remain.

I cried a key-change chorus of tears
on the hook of a ballad's broken octaves,
an all-too-familiar rhythm in my ears.
Another man dumped me on New Year's
and I believed he'd made a wreck of me,
but eventually, that particular pain always fades.
   'Goodbye to Love',
but the comfort of that song remains.

My feet first in the mosh pit
bounced to loud guitars.
   'Teenage Angst'.
I felt head-heavy with rage
which I thought would always remain,
resented all who'd dared to dent my heart,
and yet I forget what was actually said in every argument.
All that remains is the thrilling spit of punk.

When my future feels full of fear,
I blast out big beat.
    'Eat, Sleep, Rave, Repeat',
with the excitement of energetic jumping
all anxieties meet defeat.
I let go of fright.
Kiss the bass of the night.
My song's fat joy will remain

which, at home,
I replay
and replay,
and stronger than strobe lights,
my big grin remains.

People have left me
so full of emptiness,
but when my songs play
I'm not alone.

I am being held by the sound
of where I feel I belong.
I treasure my record collection.
I am saved by my songs.

Ali and Zain

Content warning: adult themes. A poem about what has happened when some modern men have met.

Ali is gay and craves getting laid. He chose to be glorious. Feels gorgeous. Fit. He has come far to this bar. Why be shy? Let's get drunk and dream. Ali expects sex although he knows one wrong word could spoil everything. Hopes dance on Ali's tongue. Ali knows clothes, every Spice Girls lyric and the correct balance of cologne with raw sweat. Other thoughts can be harmful. Come here to forget. A stranger is a friend you have not yet met. Let's lose ourselves in each other's flesh, make some memories, try to heal years of corrosive regret. Goodbye, dad. Have a nice life. No, Ali won't ever find a wife. Ali will buy any man here his next drink. Preferably a man with a really big dick.

Outside, there is a seated man. Zain is not OK. Tonight, he will sleep on the street again. Cardboard between his head and ground and the throbbing sound of pub life, club life, fit men with cash. "Excuse me, sir. Could you spare some change?" Zain feels worthless. He used to know how to swap sex for a bed, skin for a roof, until he became unfuckable. Zain has a really big dick but he does not know many Spice Girls lyrics. No cologne. Dead sweat. Sitting alone. Remembering home. Remembering his brothers. They all had really big fists. If they hit you, you stayed hit. Concrete beliefs. "Don't you love your family?" "Do you feel no shame?" Zain lost his family for one night with a man whose name he will never know, but that was ten years ago. Now, sleeping on this street is safer than any hostel. Hostels are full of fists. Hostels are full of fear. This street is lit by fit men and shining cash. Hopes dance on Zain's tongue. "Excuse me, sir. Could you spare some change?"

Inside, Ali meets Steve. Steve knows how to show the right smile to the right man but he never looks too keen. He knows how to seem a bit mean. Says he's non-scene. Muscular. Lean. He looks like a man from a magazine. He is paper-thin and glossy. Effortless cologne. No sweat. Perfect first impression. Do we need to be deep? Touch the surface. Perfect clothes. Stands close. Tactile. Magnetic smile. Listens while his eyes dance down Ali's nervous body but one wrong word could spoil everything. Steve talks like a man with a really big dick.

Ali imagines being lifted by Steve's kiss. Imagines a playful bump from Steve's thick fist. Ali imagines Steve clasping his throat. Spit in his face. Imagines the taste. Ecstatic. Ali is imagining all this when Steve suggests they go back to his.

Ali and Steve leave the bar, step outside. They meet Zain. Pouring hopes and rain. "Excuse me, sir. Could you spare some change?" Ali looks away. It is nearly the end of the day and Ali and Steve want to play. Ali is silent and Zain stinks of piss, shit clothes, unfuckable. Zain's raising voice won't leave them be. "Excuse me, sir. Could you spare some change?" Unflinching rain.

Steve is drunk. Head throbbing. Patience dropping. This street could be perfect but who is this person sitting here trying to trash that? This is not something Steve wants to see. This is not how a perfect night is meant to be. Zain shouts, "Hey! The least you could do is answer me."

No. Fuck off. Steve loses it. Fuck you. Shit. Shut the fuck up. Steve's kick splits Zain's rib. Zain screams. Broken bone. Blood soaks his cardboard home. Another kick. Steve spits in Zain's face, clasps his throat. Please. No. Another kick. *Crack.*

What will you do, Ali? How has this happened? Choose one wrong word and it spoils everything. If you wannabe a lover, don't talk too much. *Crack.* Don't mess this up, Ali. *Crack.* Ali shuts his eyes. *Crack.* Is this over yet? *Crack.* Fuck. *Crack.*

And James Lived Happily Ever After
Content warning: adult themes. A poem about a different reality.

James is like James Bond if James Bond was diabetic and from Hull. Teenage kicks. Naughty lads locked James out the changing rooms. James was naked. He did not blush. He was James Bond confident. Super sexy. He saw girls from the science block point and giggle. Inside the locked changing room, the naughty lads cackled. James just laughs too at this bare-cheeked memory from over sixty years ago.

The years since that event have become a blur in James' happy head. He does remember wetting himself in the nursery school play, and at secondary when he met the Duchess of Kent, and when those naughty lads locked James out of the changing rooms.

When his daughter sees him smile, she doesn't always know why. She'll try to smile too. She holds his hand. She didn't know he was her dad until she was an adult. Now she is an adult, he doesn't know he is her dad. She cries when her own mind locks her out and for weeks she cannot visit.

"Did I tell you I met the Duchess of Kent yesterday?" are the first words James will say when his daughter returns from months away and sometimes his daughter is the Duchess of Kent or sometimes his daughter is his mum or teacher when he wets himself and he never remembers he once had a wife.

At night, James strides from bed, naked. Sits, star-lit in the lounge. James Bond confident. A James Bond movie marathon is on the communal lounge TV. Perfect. A man on a mission. Live and let die.

Nineteen years failing to get that promotion is now forgotten. He no longer thinks angry thoughts about his boss. He doesn't even remember having a boss. He doesn't know his life savings were spent living in this care home, but he knows the people in this home do care. His wife's family never liked him, but now they don't live in his happy head. James' mind is so full of love, he let go of those thoughts that never mattered and they aren't even worth a goodbye. He does not feel fright because what's the worst thing that could happen? Girls from the science block pointing and giggling?

James Bond is a secret agent who may have forgotten his mission. That does not mean his mission was not a success.

Isolation

Haiku for Loss

Fall for my cold phone.
With mishaps on the wrong apps,
love is uninstalled.

8-Bit Buddy

A 'NES' is a 'Nintendo Entertainment System'; a video game console from the 1980s. '8-Bit' refers to the technological power of that console, which by today's standards is not very great. All the characters referenced here are characters from Nintendo games, except for the characters in one line. Top points for you if you know which characters are not Nintendo characters!

My mates can't wait to forget me.
Berate my state because I can't play correctly
the latest games, but get my NES and I will be
your Greatest 8-Bit Buddy – if you let me

make our lives easy wherever we go.
I'll be the Luigi to your Mario.
Your comrade. Your helper. Whatever you think.
Can I be your Zelda? Would you be my Link?
Tomorrow's long trails will feel laconic.
I'll follow like Tails 'cos you're Super Sonic.
Wherever you long for I'll get us there sooner.
Will you, Donkey Kong, take my Donkey Kong Jr?

My mates can't wait to forget me.
Berate my state because I can't play correctly
the latest games, but get my NES and I will be
your Greatest 8-Bit Buddy – if you let me

join the best at Dragon Quest.
You're mega, man. I'd be blessed
to press your B Button. You bet this
means even more than my high score at Tetris.
I'll steer you clear if spears appear
on Chip 'n Dale or Metal Gear.

Let me be a buddy on whom you depend.
It's my final fantasy to find a friend.

My mates can't wait to forget me.
Berate my state because I can't play correctly
the latest games, but get my NES and I will be
your Greatest 8-Bit Buddy – if you let me.

Video Games Don't Hurt Me

Shining Force is a video game from the '16-bit' era (more recent than '8-bit', but still old as the hills!). The Shining Force series is my personal favourite series of video games.

Video games don't hurt me.
People do.
Why would I risk the pain
of trusting someone new

when I feel safe alone at home?
There's nothing I like more
than playing video games I've played
a hundred times before.

Everything's familiar.
Here, I know my goal.
No lies. No tears. No anger.
Here, I'm in control.

In the second Shining Force,
there is this bit I found,
not part of the main game:
it's a village, underground,

where dwarves forge special items.
They toil ceaselessly.
Together. Comrades. Family.
A true community.

Playing this is easy.
I barely need to try.
I know these dwarves won't leave me.
Don't hurt me with "Goodbye".

OK, it's true, I'd share this game
if anyone would care,
but I can't risk rejection
so I'm not going there.

I think this game's my favourite,
with its subterranean crew.
It fills a space that's empty,
sat without my Player Two.

Pantoum for Possibilities

Content warning: adult themes. Another poem about staring at a screen. A pantoum is a series of verses where the second line of a verse comes becomes the first line in the next verse, and the fourth line in one becomes the third of the next too. (I could call a block of poetry a 'stanza', not a 'verse', but I like the word 'verse' more.)

Must my eyes lock on mobile screens?
Entrapped online. Cows killed on film.
The slaughterhouse. What happens next?
Reflecting eyes stare back. En-caged,

entrapped, online, cows killed on film.
I watch until my screen turns black.
Reflecting eyes stare back, en-caged,
and then my phone lights up again.

I watch until the screen turns black.
No sleep. I think of activists,
and then my phone lights up again.
I'm not like them. I'm trapped, online.

No sleep. I think of activists.
Do most men not care? Someone, say
I'm not like them. I'm trapped, online,
but not forever. Things could change.

Do most men not care? Someone, say
my hands could help. This world is cruel,
but not forever. Things could change.
Where is the key to set life free?

My hands could help. This world is cruel.
Must my eyes lock on mobile screens?
Where is the key to set life free?
The slaughterhouse. What happens next?

People Like Shit
Content warning: adult themes.

He hopes that his jokes melt the snowflakes.
He's telling his truth with his wit
and punchlines to beat the oppressors,
but he does not treat people like shit.

Online, he is loud, for the underdog.
Those Twitter trolls just don't get it.
This man stands against cancel culture.
He does not treat people like shit.

The tears flood his face when a movie
shows cruelty to some sad misfit.
He cries because he knows compassion.
Why do folks treat people like shit?

He listens to lyrics. Loves Bowie
and Pixies (before their first split).
Has stripes on his arm from the blade marks.
His music makes him feel less shit.

He won't say he misses his sister.
At school, they were regularly hit
by first older kids, then their parents
or uncle when he'd babysit.

Framed photo of dad. That's a strong man.
His family is really close-knit.
These kids nowadays should be tougher.
Don't be a thin-skinned little shit.

He's kept the same shirt for a decade.
It's part of a perfect outfit.
He's handsome. He has a high sex drive,
but most dates just treat him like shit.

No women or men really like him.
They don't get his depth or his grit.
The pretty ones only shag alphas.
Successful men. People like shit.

When raging, he punches a pillow.
Smokes weed so he doesn't lose it.
Can't stand refugees or the homeless.
He's dignified. He's not a shit.

He's proud that he isn't some scrounger.
Gets drunk every night, but could quit.
The beggars on spice make his blood boil.
He'd never touch that kind of shit.

Last night, he went out to a party.
His neighbours claim he threw a fit.
Said, "Racism isn't a real thing,
just people treat people like shit."

He's done lots of research on YouTube.
His laptop at midnight, moonlit,
shares blogs that confirm his opinions.
Most people treat people like shit.

His housemate says, "Work on your anger,"
but he won't be a hypocrite.
Tonight is the night. He will fight back
and never again feel like shit.

Five Days Dreaming of Sleep
Content warning: adult themes.

1

He could be happy when he makes a brew. Who needs spoons? The coffee jar is tipped. Bountiful brown granules cascade, a monochrome rainbow shades the day.

He could be happy because insomnia means more time to enjoy TV. Keep going. Yes life. A 1AM documentary on oxbow lakes takes his brain to a beautiful place and the curve of a smile cuts his face.

He could be happy because doctors say he is not ill. Being told you are not ill is a good thing, right? Maybe that means these horrible head pains might one day ... just go away. Need for sleep might one day ... just go away. Flashbacks of the knife against his neck might one day ... who knows?

Sleep is nothing but a fistful of frightening nightmares but when he is awake, he can choose to look cheerful.

2

The nice woman was shocked to spot him emptying a sack of crumpled, crumby crisp packets over the grass outside the church.

Why? He has been the most attentive member of the Litter Picking Brigade. No one else has spoken more passionately about the need to clean these streets than him. No one else has attended more litter picking mornings than him. So ... why?

He can't answer. The truth feels grimy inside his mind. Some thoughts, once spoken, become too messy to ever pick back up again and tidy away and he does want to be tidy, but if these streets were clean, no litter left to pick, where would he go? Who would he see? Who would he be?

Keep going. Yes life. Lack of sleep means arriving early for these meetings is more than a joy. These mornings outside the church are sacred. He prays that they will never end.

3

Beneath the blind, balanced on his window ledge, he has made three towers of twenty, fifty and ten pence pieces. Not great at counting. He can walk shop aisles for hours adding up what he thinks he can afford, but always the checkout girl must ask what he wants to leave behind.

Beneath his boxer-shorts, he has three shadowy bruises left by the mugger whose fingers slid inside these damp pants whilst pressing a knife to his neck. Nails. Lips. Fists. Blood. Not great at countering. Recounting this story to his doctor is not enough to earn him any therapy.

Beneath closed eyes, those rare moments of sleep bring one of three recurring dreams. There's the dream where he falls silently into factory machinery, innards split by spiky cogs. There's the dream where he has earned his freedom from this old tower block, fingertips shine like bright silver coins, feet leave concrete and he can fly for hours. Great at flying. Keep going. Yes life. There's the dream where the knife goes in and out and in and out and always the checkout girl must ask what he wants to leave behind.

4

He loves this local shop. The checkout girl smiles. When it's not busy, they chat wonderfully about nothing. Keep going. Yes life. Nothing is full of warmth.

It sounds silly to place such value on moments spent with a stranger who is paid to be there, but that's what he comes here for.

This girl from the checkout saw him at the bus stop yesterday and without hesitation gently threw over a healing hello which he caught with eager ears. That one word helped him get through another day in a job where people say hello, but don't seem to mean anything by it. On the long weeks where repeated sleepless nights have left him muffling screams into his spit-wet pillow, sometimes a healing hello can mean everything.

When travelling home, he often goes to the shop to get a tin of anything and genuine friendliness.

5

At 5AM, here are some people he could contact.

His dad never texts back, but family is everything, isn't it? He must message him but never have expectations.

Then there is that person from work. He fantasises about what their fevered fumblings might be like. Even sexier than finding 5AM porn on his phone. Sometimes, some mornings, he has seen this person being mean to people at the bus stop, but that's just modern humour, isn't it? This person would never be mean to him, would they? He has this person's number and sends another message but doesn't get anything back and that's modern life and that is fine.

Then there is a stranger in an Amazon warehouse working many miles away. He messages when he buys another thing he doesn't need, but he saw it on sale so that's a good deal, isn't it?

Then there is the woman at the church and there is the checkout girl who have both been nice, but how would they feel if he sapped their fun with self-pitying sorrow? Don't message them.

If he did get to sleep right now, right this second, he would get at least two full hours' rest before the morning alarm.

Wide-eyed fantasies.

If he ended it all, if he did take that knife, finally felt it really inside, how would that feel? No more surface slices. Push it in. This could be his time to finally make a definite decision. His dad would be disappointed, wouldn't he? Wouldn't he? He couldn't do that to dad. Subtle cuts give just enough physical pain to drain feeling.

After he has put the knife away, he sends some more messages, just saying 'Hi'. Keep going. Yes life. He wonders whether this time, someone might reply.

Goodbye, Anxiety

Content warning: adult themes.

I want to try to say goodbye
to Anxiety.

Be free
of stress.

Yes,
I know we sometimes need to feel fear.
If a fierce tiger leapt in here
I'd want my fight or flight,
but that's quite
different from viscous voices at night
in my head, predicting dread.
In my bed, I stare out my window,
up to the stars.
Dwell on past pain.
Counting scars.
Predict hurt.
Sleepless. Alert.
I try my best to rest,
but too often find
Anxiety tip-toes back to my mind.

Awake. Alone. I look to my phone.
A gleaming screen to ease this scene.

My finger taps
on apps
to locate friends,
but then my phone sends
endless conflict.
Endless hate.

Kim kicking off at snowflake Kate.
James blames Nate for making him late.
Luke accuses Sarah of having an affair
when Sarah shares
party pics with unknown men there.
Mark calls Nadia racist.
Jen calls Jonny gay.
Don't be ignorant, Dominic.
Don't you look away.

Then, adverts target my insecurities.
This cream clears all your impurities.
Subscribe to Happy App
to make you feel less glum.
Buy things to prove
you still love your mum.

None of this helps me unwind.
Need to find
focus,
fix my mind.

I feel my phone laugh
at my chosen path.
Calls me daft.
Is my phone too smart?

Panic is pulling me apart.
How do I start
to stop
these fears from flowing?

I try to say "Goodbye",
but my Anxiety is not going.

Love in the Sea

From loneliness to solitude. A rewrite of a poem called 'Heal', originally written for Shada Aziz Iqbal, based on her experiences, for Manchester International Festival.

Look down.
With toes submerged in ocean foam,
I escape
into idyllic isolation.
No longer lonely.
Simply solitary.
I leave being me
without taking a single step.
Hear land-lapping waves.
Smell salt.
A sharp nip in the air.
Place a finger to lips and
see the vast horizon.
Stare into ever changing shades of blues.
Kick bad habits
standing here.

Look up.
Every cloud has its rhythm.
There are soft, white billows
on welcoming, sunny days.
Sometimes, there are beautiful storms
with passions of thunder.
I don't ever see a sky as being too angry.
I love lightning.
Every emotion can heal.
This is a healing place,
only the faintest outline of rock
beyond the mist.

There is so much above
and so much so deeply beneath
where sea reflects sky and
sky reflects sea.

Here,
life is where all can peacefully be.

Companionship

Haiku for Friends

Dark winters, alone.
Friends text my cold phone. Light smiles.
Their jokes bring bright beams.

Sestina for Friends

A sestina is a poem with six verses of six lines each, and then a final three lines. All the verses have the same six words at the ends of their lines but in six different sequences. Dedicated to my friend Graeme.

I'm forty now. I have fantastic friends.
We once were lads with plastic blades as toys.
We made our He-Man action figures fight.
Saw heroes and their great comrades unite.
On Central Road, I still recall the place
where all our best adventures used to be.

Those days are gone. The boy I used to be
has grown with help from all my awesome friends.
They focus and direct me to a place
where I'm as joyful as a boy with toys.
I love it when my friends and I unite.
We are a team who will win any fight.

But why did He-Man ever want to fight?
He made the world a fairer place to be.
He'd face injustice. Bravely he'd unite
with Teela, Stratos, Ram Man … all his friends
with morals deeper than just tiny toys.
But can I make the world a better place?

I see some kids get told to know their place.
In council homes, I see teenagers fight.
They don't use plastic blades. No, these aren't toys.
These kids are told that they will always be
the chavs the middle-class won't want as friends.
Communities too diff'rent to unite.

But what if diff'rent people did unite?
When kids are taught they ought to know their place
can conflict kill the chance of being friends?
Is it naive to not expect a fight?
Is there a way for adult minds to be
as carefree as young children with their toys?

I think there's wisdom in my He-Man toys.
A firm belief that people can unite
whatever their backstories seem to be,
and yes, we'll make the world a fairer place.
We'll challenge those who say that we must fight.
We'll prove that we are better when we're friends,

when kids find joy from any starting place,
when council-housed and middle-class unite.
The world's a better place when full of friends.

My Friend, Online

Not everything online is bad. A great mate I met at tae kwon-do became a wonderful online gaming companion when lockdown kept us physically apart. Dedicated to my friend Scott.

At home, I play a game that's trending.
Wish this game was never-ending.
I've been hurt, but this game's mending
me 'til I feel fine.
Yes, mate!
I'm online.

At work, I don't enjoy the present.
Winter mornings. Moon's a crescent.
Daydreaming of when life's pleasant,
where my time is mine;
with my mate,
he waits online.

I see my boss peripherally.
I know what she expects from me.
I give her what she wants to see:
a construct she'll define.
Standing by,
we are offline.

When I play games, I'm real. No doubt.
It's here, I know what life's about.
I wish I could exist without
a world that can confine
with broken smiles
which glitch offline.

I play these games, my nerves untwist.
We rank each title. Here's a list!
We are the kings of Iron Fist.
My Playstation's a shrine.
Let's go, mate!
I'm online!

We play our games and bad thoughts scatter.
Who's the winner? Does it matter?
Online friendships never shatter.
Feel our smiles combine.
I'm alive.
I'm online.

Warmth: A Poem About a Pandemic

True story from the early days of coronavirus.

Icy silence fills this window.
The usual laughter of children playing
and families chattering outside
has withdrawn from my world.

Don't think about bills.
Don't turn up my radiator.
Fetch the blue jumper granddad knitted before his 90th
and imagine what he'd have made of all this lockdown malarkey.

Unexpectedly, my phone's tone splits the quiet
and I realise
I have not spoken one word all day.

"Hello?"

It is a cold call salesperson,
a stranger breaking into my evening
and releasing sounds from my mouth
I hadn't realised I had trapped.

I don't want to buy anything, except
I would please like a friendly chat.
I would like that,
and although I know

telesales protocol does not encourage sparkling camaraderie
between trader and would-be customer,
for a few seconds, this uninvited humanity fills me
with warmth.

My Northern Soul

A poem originally written for Shanny, based on his experiences, for Manchester International Festival.

Marvin Gaye would say he heard it on the grapevine.
Curtis Mayfield's 'Move On Up' makes me feel fine.
Great Stone Hotel, Cellar Club, Temptations' 'Cloud Nine'.
I love jazz, rock 'n' roll,
Motown and Northern Soul.

Need to go out dancing. Wear black brogue Italian shoes.
Shirts with yellow piping are the shirts I like to choose
to match my mohair trousers of the brightest royal blues.
My brother John first told
me of Northern Soul.

The Moss Side men. The lads from school. We haven't got a care.
Dennis, Harry, David, and the music we all share.
The tunes that lift us and the friendship that is always there.
Tonight, we know our goal.
We dance to Northern Soul.

When Martha Reeves is singing, you can't help but sway and jerk.
The head goes where it wants to whilst the legs do all the work.
For all my life, music has made my spirits perk.
I dance, and I am whole.
Here, with Northern Soul.

From a Glastonbury Mosh Pit

My first poem written as Glastonbury Festival Poet in Residence.

It is five in the morning.
Two people
feel neck-skin prickles
under soft summer solstice sunrise,
deep
in a Glastonbury mosh pit.
As bass-lines boom
through thousands of bouncing feet
searching for a place to stand,
two people find love.

Keisha shares water with Kaz.
Spilling laughter.
It is Keisha's first festival,
so she carries enough smiles
to inspire a nation.
Can repeat line-up times
like children recite times tables.
Has drawn routes to stages
on backs of hands
like maps on pages
of folklore fables.

Grin-soaked,
Kaz drinks this water and decides:
forget the office.
Being with Keisha
means more to Kaz
than team-building workmates
who knock down dreams.

Kaz and Keisha met five minutes ago
and now
their friendship is deeper than time.

Here.
They have found exactly where they will stand.
From pitching tents to their first band,
from raves to campaigns of good will,
from folks who'll chill to jokes that thrill,
from protest art of paint and steel
to juggled flames and healing fields.

Imagine
if Kaz and Keisha's feelings
could be bottled and shared.

Make our thirsty nations drunk on love.
Cheers refuelled at the mosh pit stop.
Voices flowing in free music streams.
Excited minds, dripping with dreams.

Glastonbury Mud

Another poem written as Glastonbury Festival Poet in Residence.

I do not know your name.

In Glastonbury, we are all defined by
mud.

Through rain, we dance,
our names sliding off into
mud.

Waltzing wellies
leave imprints of laughter
across druid-drenched earth.

When Björk sang
"It takes courage to enjoy it",
I'm sure she was singing about
Glastonbury mud.

It took courage for me to enjoy these
thousands of
voices cheering
when all I'd ever known
from loud crowds
was anxiety and beatings.

I had learned to fear
voices shouting.
My blood on their fists.
Would hide at home,
inside my headphones,
break beats, not war,
Mars as a girl,

red-faced and scared of the world,
scared of names hurled,
stuck to me.
Mucky.
Men calling me dirty.
Filthy queer.
Unclean names.

You do not know my names.
In Glastonbury, we are all defined by
mud.

Through rain, we dance,
our names sliding off into
mud.

Now
my voice joins
this applauding chorus,
thousands
in rain-coated androgyny's
ecstatic,
grounded
harmony

because

we are courage,

we are joy,

we *are* dirty,

we *are* filthy,

we *are* mud.

Ghazal for Possibilities

A ghazal is an Arabic poetry form, often about loss, with no fewer than five verses of two lines each, many lines ending in the same word. Often the author puts their own name in the final verse. Dedicated to Josh.

Piles of vegan candy at a festival where the sweets are free.
I see my sweet companions, who campaign to save lives not yet
   free.

Piles of pamphlets and leaflets show how cows in crates are
   pumped with drugs.
The calves are dragged from drained mothers, killed for milk,
   and never free.

I find reminding myself how animals are kept upsets me.
Unfocused, I fall from my feet – *crash!* – all of my leaflets fly free.

My dear, kind friend helps me, gathering up my leaflets and
   dropped thoughts.
We stop and talk – of how cows die for sweets – and lament those
   not free.

He says, "Dom, there are piles of possibilities, and we can help.
It's a great start for you and me to give these vegan sweets for
   free."

High-fiving Tree Branches

A poem originally written for Saba Mirshafiei, based on her experiences, for Manchester International Festival.

Things have been a bit different around our tree this past year. Even the insects noticed. They buzz about beneath me, less bothered by people. The parakeets squeak even more confidently above. They've never been the quietest neighbours.

I've always been wary of people. Small kids chase you. I heard one man say I *"looked tasty"*. That's not good, right?

There is one woman who makes the strangest noises. I think she thinks she's speaking my language. I like that she tries. She always wears the same coat, and brings the best nuts. I'm talking cashews.

I have never touched a person's hand before. She is kind.

How could I not feel happy when I saw her running laps around my park? High-fiving tree branches. You could see she did not find running easy, but I don't believe that there was anyone here who didn't share her joy. Even the parakeets cheered. I wished I could have cheered too. I just watched. Cheered inside my head.

I don't know her name, but I felt proud, seeing her using this weird year to do something good.

I hear others call her Squirrel Woman.

I wish there was a way to let her know how happy she makes me.

Rondeau for When I'm Low

A rondeau is a poetry form based on two rhyme sounds. This rondeau is dedicated to Luiz.

I'm like your plants. When I am low,
I love the light that you bestow.
Your brown eyes shine. You glow with glee.
Into your home, you've welcomed me.
It's where the air knows laughter's flow.

Your jokes will warm me, top-to-toe.
There's life that thrives from roots below.
The plants get water. We share tea.
I'm like your plants.

I'm nourished where I love to go.
Into your tender care. I know
there's nowhere else I'd like to be.
Into your heart, you've welcomed me.
My life is greater.

Here,

I grow.

I'm like your plants.

Sonnet for Shell

A sonnet is a poetry form with fourteen lines, usually having ten syllables in each line. Dedicated to Michelle.

Some children can't control the things they do.
They sometimes scream and sob or hit and bite.
But there's a special school where they have you
and when their world is dark, you are their light.

Our government control and what they do
won't make it easy, but you do stay bright.
Despite the bite of funding cuts, there's you;
still glowing, growing, when their grip is tight.

Your patience, love and kindness shining through.
Then, after work, we meet. A true delight.
You say you're low, but jokes and laughs with you
are greater than with most folks at their height.

I treasure all the time you spend with me.
You make my world a brighter place to be.

A Frisbee
Dedicated to Nick.

Nick throws me
his frisbee.
I miss it
completely.

Under the sun's golden rays,
eight of us have met to play a game
for Nick's birthday.

Nick
is quick,
flicking a frisbee with fantastic skill,
but still,
it is a throw which I fumble.
The frisbee tumbles
from my trembling fingers to grassy ground
with a clunking sound.
I've lost count
of the amount
of throws I've failed to catch.
This is no formal match.
Just a few friends spending time together
in a park.
Nick is a spectacularly sparky guy,
so it's no wonder why
everyone
finds Nick fun.

Nick is someone who is super at several sports,
but never plays fiercely.

When I fumble the frisbee,
he is there to assist me.
Though others catch better,
he will never dismiss me.
When I doubt myself,
he is there to convince me
he's pleased that I'm playing.
Though I'm never nifty,
with all of Nick's friends,
he is gleeful and giddy.

Supportive. Inclusive.
In complete opposition
to the kids back at school
in constant competition.

For back at my school, all sports would mean
me being picked last for every team.
The lads picked on me. They'd make such a fuss.
"Does Dom have to play with us?"
Whatever the sport, the response was the same.
The nerd was not welcome for any game.

But now, that's in the distant past.
I don't want to make those memories last.

However many throws I miss, Nick throws me a grin.
I never doubt this is a game which I am welcome in,
because Nick has a frisbee which he keeps on giving,
and the way that Nick plays is a great way for living.
It doesn't matter if I make a mistake.
Nick gives more than he'll ever take.

There's no need for scores. Nick makes it clear.
The best part of this game is us just being here.

Like Puppies
Dedicated to Ian.

... and we are like puppies, the way that we play.
Our happiness holding the weight of the day.
We're two cheeky mongrels; the wild and the stray,
and we are like puppies, the way that we play.

Our happiness holding the moments we share,
for we are like puppies (despite our lost hair),
and all days are better when I know you're there.
Our happiness holding the moments we share.

We're two silly mongrels, the stray and the wild.
We laugh away troubles. Life's easy and mild.
For twenty years, you've kept the joy of a child.
We're two silly mongrels, the stray and the wild,

and we are like puppies, our games never end.
There's never been pain which your presence can't mend.
You're loyal and awesome. You're this man's best friend.
... and we are like puppies, our games never end.

ex nunc

I Am

For today.

It's sunny. I am running.
In the park, two puppies play.
I see a bird fly close to me,
then watch it fly away.

There's rhythm to my running,
grounding rhythm in my feet.
A thought is coming close to me.
I'm feeling my heart beat.

This thought calls me a loser and
this thought tells me I'm cursed.
This thought predicts a future where
this thought says *fear the worst*.

The ones you love will leave you and
you will break down and cry
and no one else will care when
they all die or say goodbye.

I see this thought fly close to me
then watch it fly away.
I let it go. I know the truth.
I watch the puppies play.

I'm here. I am not stress or fear.
I'm here. I am not rage.
I'm here. I am not sorrow.
My feelings aren't a cage.

I am the rhythm of a breath.
The puppies race and bark.
The air is soft. The sun shines on
the games played in the park,

and when I watch the puppies play,
their joy is all I see.
I share a rhythm with today.
A perfect place to be.

My Friend, Sleep
For tonight.

I lie with my reality.
Sleep once felt so far from me.
I needed Sleep so desperately,
but rest felt like a fantasy.

Alone in winter, when it's the most cold.
The icy nights' howling can't be controlled.
I've screamed into pillows. Recall when I'd weep
whilst cursing another night left without Sleep.

My mind felt frozen and strangled by strife.
But winter will end. There will be a new life.
Who am I now? What do I bring
to embrace a new cycle and start fresh in spring?

What is an insomniac? What is my identity?
I have kept treating my Sleep like an enemy,
like an attack, I have tried to defend.
I never thought I might treat Sleep like a friend.

If Sleep was my friend, I have not been that nice.
I've cursed Sleep's departure more than once or twice.
I've sobbed and I've shouted when Sleep ceased to be.
So why would my Sleep want to be close to me?

If I was my Sleep, why would I choose to spend
my nights with a guy who won't call me a friend?
With Sleep so insulted through all of my day,
by night, I'm unsettled, and Sleep stays away.

Can I calm down? Can I not sob or shout?
Can I be the kind of guy Sleep wants about?
When I need to rest, do I know who I'll be?
Be kind to Sleep. Let Sleep be with me.

This is the moment. Straight from this date,
I'm choosing to treat meeting Sleep like a mate.
We're friends. There's no conflict. I welcome this guest.
I welcome this moment. I welcome rest.

Haiku for a New Season

Love is who we are.
Breakfasts, there to share with friends,
where dreams spring to life.

TALKBACK

THE UNOFFICIAL AND UNAUTHORISED
DOCTOR WHO INTERVIEW BOOK

VOLUME THREE: THE EIGHTIES